RANCHER

TEXT
Selah Saterstrom

IMAGES
H.C. Dunaway Smith

BURROW PRESS | ORLANDO, FL

First printed in limited edition hardcover, 2021
Text © Selah Saterstrom, pocket edition 2023
Art © H.C. Dunaway Smith
Book + Cover Design: Ryan Rivas
Published by Burrow Press
ISBN: 978-1-941681-27-5

In Place of a Forward

Basket Poem #13 (from *The Friend* series)

I make a basket a choral basket I ask I ask I go in I enter in

am amongst we are and are inky perfumed shelves of veils

descending in pitch dark inside the velvet of the weeping

hole that blinks

> We will find a place where one can rest,
>
> where a story can rest.

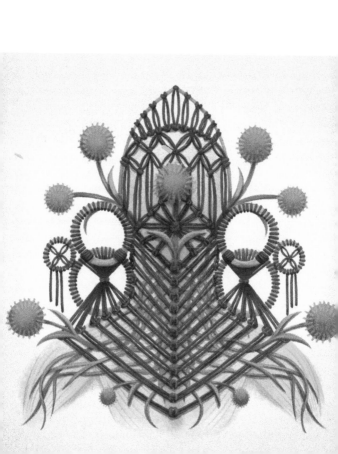

My rapist bought a house with a swimming pool in El Paso.

One issue I'm having while writing this essay is that I have nothing interesting to say about rape. Not even my own(s). And I literally just started writing this essay.

My friend, however, is harvesting black widow spider eggs and putting the egg sacs in her freezer. I learned this news from another, mutual friend. Meanwhile, I have said nothing to my egg sac harvesting friend about her habit.

I attempt to research the egg sac harvesting process, but only learn how to kill black widow spiders. People love the "vacuum cleaner method." Though, "in such cases one should also take the vacuum bag out immediately, place it in a securely tied garbage bag and place it in a dumpster, preferably not located on your property." This author grimly continues, "Trying to crush or squash the egg sacs may release a flurry of tiny little baby spiders, which you will probably be unable to catch in time."

Speaking with the mutual friend who told me about this situation, we discuss our amazement at our other friend's delicate work of egg harvesting. We imagine the sacs. Encaustic yellowed, detached testicles, furred, but internally. I tell my friend that though I guess our other friend is trying to freeze the babies to death, it also feels like a sort of resurrection spell.

My OCD catches on and I begin to think about the black widow spider and the egg sacs. The thoughts get wild. This intensity builds for several weeks. This is a thinking-type beyond curiosity and feels more like infestation.

Later, the Internet tells me spider eggs cannot survive being frozen and that there is no danger of the eggs defrosting and hatching.

But I know what I know, don't you? You know, too. We know. We have bodies and death and fecundity strung up between the stakes throughout. Nothing means not one thing, a plurality of intensities. *Wherever there is nothing*, Diderot wrote, *read that I love you*. Diderot, who died of pulmonary thrombosis during an overheated Parisian summer in 1784, whose corpse, disinterred by grave robbers, was smeared in greasy vestiges across church flooring.

Stilled things hatch when the conditions become conducive.

So I know what I know. Don't you?

Diderot was especially concerned with the questions: What is sex? and, How should we appreciate art?

In graduate school the young award-winning professor handed us a Ray Carver book. Choke on this beauty, he said while looking like he knew a secret that rhymed with the word tits.

One issue I'm having while writing this essay is that I have nothing interesting to say about rape.

Though I can imagine a cruel sentence.

I can imagine a syntax that performs itself with such precision that in its achievement it eradicates into a trace within the ongoing crime scene.

I can imagine a syntax that, like a marvelous firework, explodes in an orchestrated design afterimaging into an inky dark: a sentence that transmutes into its content.

I can imagine writing as a Eucharistic event. In the mouth. In house. I can imagine a sentence which punches me in the stomach, the soft middle. I can imagine the emergent gut freshly loosed, which opens its weeping hole.

I do not want the ideally achieved sentence about rape. I do not want rape as a narrative device.

Additionally, my rapist is not interesting.

With the exception of mating season, black widow spiders are solitary. Females live up to three years and males, one or two months due to sexual cannibalism. After mating, killing, and eating their sex partners, females create sacs containing between 200 and 900 eggs that hatch in a month's time. The hatched babies are cannibals and eat each other. Few survive.

What a bunch of fucking cannibals these spiders are! I say to my friend who told me about the egg sac situation. Horrifying, she 100% agrees. Then one day I learn that the mother spider is gone. Just gone. Oh my god! I exclaim and then demand to know what happened though nobody knows. I know! friend says, I goddamned know that shit.

I never bring up the spider again. But here I am, all this time later, writing about it. I have never stopped writing about it from the moment it came into existence for me.

Slick spindle legs tip-tap the pink sponged meat of a heart, then enter with an in-breath, sink. Elsewhere, a butterfly caged in a human mouth batters itself to death.

"Resurrection: A Short Story"
by S Saterstrom

for Larry

So one day Lazarus and Diderot are sitting in a bar.

Diderot: Have you heard the one about the East Berliners and the bananas? After the wall came down, people in East Berlin got to knowing about bananas. Before, they never really knew about bananas.

One day a banana starts running like crazy, a frenzied mob of East Berliners in hot pursuit. The banana ducks into an alley where he meets a kiwi. Jesus, Banana says, you'd better get ready; we can't hide anymore. Ha! says the kiwi in a clever, knowing way, and then does a fancy dance and departs with haste, the banana just standing there like a dope.

That was the joke people told, variations of it, after the war.

Lazarus: That's pretty good. The banana just standing there like that.

I keep meaning to tell the story of my black widow spider obsession to my friend who lived with the black widow spider in the first place. She is an organized and thorough person and between us I imagine we have, at this point, read most everything about black widow spiders. We have ideas to exchange. I imagine doing this in the presence of our other friend, the one who first told me about the entire situation, the three of us together, laughing. In this dream, we are safe and have what is needed.

One thing that may not be obvious to the reader is that I have been writing this essay for a long time. The world this essay began in is not the world in which it will end.

What is rape's relation to pandemics?

The correlation between epidemics and pandemics and violence against women has not been well documented. Still, we can look to events such as the Ebola epidemic peak in 2014. Dr. Seema Yasmin, a physician and former epidemiologist at the Centers for Disease Control and Prevention, notes that we are only now understanding that Liberia, Sierra Leone, and Guinea saw a surge in teenage pregnancies caused by an increase of rape during that epidemic. For example, the teenage pregnancy rate in Sierra Leone increased 65%. Another pained detail: In Liberia, 10% of children who lost at least one parent to Ebola were forced into sex work.

Outbreaks of infectious diseases leave girls and women—particularly girls and women of color—more vulnerable to violence and rape. In the United States, based on patterns witnessed during and after the economic crisis of 2008, 9/11, and Hurricanes Sandy and Katrina, experts declared that the Coronavirus would result in escalated violence of every sort against girls and women. According to the United Nations in March of 2020, "Pandemics make existing gender inequalities for women and girls worse, and can impact how they receive treatment and care."

What does capitalism have to do with our rapes? Everything. A national lack of infrastructure, as revealed by every disaster, ensures it.

Capitalism was in the soggy corner of the room; it was in the acrid dog piss-saturated carpet. It was in the polyester slick of the popped, fitted sheet. It was in the clean angle of morning when another day began.

Capitalism is in the soggy corner of the room, it is in the acrid dog piss saturated carpet. It is in the polyester slick of the popped, fitted sheet. It is in the clean angle of morning as another day begins.

The house was a respectable rancher with a pool, wife, and two kids active in sports programs at their Catholic school. And Raper doesn't look that bad, sort of like a puffy Eddie Vedder in a track suit, not remarkable, but it could be worse. At any rate, he seems grateful for everything now.

I notice a poolside pic of his daughter at her fourteenth birthday.

It's a hard age, fourteen.

When I was her age, in the moments before her dad would rape me and/or oversee my rape by others, he called me Orca, as in, his words, a fat ass whale. Everyone thought it was hilarious. I laughed, too.

I lived in a situation where there was often not enough food. For most of junior high, I ate day old Piggly Wiggly Bear Claws—four for a dollar—and smoked cigarettes. I would try and spread out the Bear Claws, but would usually still eat all four in a frenzy. Then I'd cry. Then I'd light a Doral Full Flavor.

Where I lived, there wasn't enough of anything, including oversight, so rapers slipped in. Terror rewires those it overtakes. Did you know that the terrorized laugh more than most?

It is true that my disdain for my rapist includes the fact that the rancher has a swimming pool, something I have wanted for myself my entire life.

While working on a different part of this essay, I realize that I have also been writing a novella about Helen of Troy which features a swimming pool. The novella is based on a memory of discovering an abandoned swimming pool in which an alligator lived. I was a girl at the time of this discovery, and later that same day my mother got drunk and told everyone at the restaurant to look where the alligator had bitten her, meaning her vagina, which she dramatically swatted in a Mae West-like fashion.

Other true stories about swimming pools include the time my wife and I were late-night swimming in a 100-year-old stone pool in a decaying hot springs resort in a rural Colorado mountain town when all of the sudden, a thick fog enveloped the pool and we sensed the murmuring of many voices; the time my best friend and I went skinny dipping in an enchanted swimming pool in New Orleans that provided psychedelic glories (was the pool somehow full of mushroom tea?); and the motel swimming pool in rural Idaho where I brought my infant daughter into the cold, cold waters.

Why do the terrorized laugh?

During graduate school, I scribble this question in the margins of my notes while doing field visits to genocidal sites and interviewing former inmates and soldiers of genocidal regimes. Judging by my notebooks, it is a question that came up for me in Poland, Cambodia, and later in Tibetan refugee resettlement villages in the Himalayas of Northern India near the border with Pakistan.

I see archival photos of people laughing while being terrorized. Such laughing people are mentioned during my interviews and discussions.

Those recalling the laughing people share how, at the time, they believed those people insane; people broken by the weight of cruelty. Though now, every person who recalls such individuals no longer believes they were insane. They believe they were prophets.

Scientists call the laughter of terrified people "fearful laughter" and they do not know why people sometimes laugh while in a state of terror.

One theory suggests laughter is inherently social, which is to say that when we laugh, we are signaling to those around us. This theory says that fearful laughter is an expression of submission. In such instances laughter both admits fear and communicates a desire to circumvent conflict.

Another theory posits that fearful laughter represents a denial of fear. We are scared, but we are also trying to convince ourselves and others we are not. Another theory submits that we are trying to rewrite our horror as manageable, that it might be endured.

Another theory argues that incongruous responses help us to regulate emotions. In such cases when one is overwhelmed by an emotion, expressing what is considered to be the opposite emotion can help restore emotional balance. Another theory states that we laugh because horror and humor have, at their core, the same motor: transgression.

Another theory says people who laugh at inappropriate times are sociopaths.

I try to find my rapist's place of employment. Based on the name I'm working with, three people present as options: a young, regionally famous athlete, a Border Patrol Agent, and a prison guard. I know there is no way he is the athlete and shudder at the two remaining options, both of which seem like appropriate fits. After more sleuthing, I conclude he is neither. In fact, I can find no record of his current life outside of a very small social media presence. I was curious. I had been thinking of ways I might take my revenge.

When I first saw the photograph of him standing in front of the rancher with its swimming pool, I had a psychotic break made possible by RTS (Rape Trauma Syndrome), a complex post-traumatic stress disorder. During a psychotic break, a person has the overwhelming sensation that there is no external correlate to one's internal experience of radical flux. One loses the ability to sequence thoughts and becomes "disordered." All kinds of troubling affects can result, ranging from mild to extreme.

Sometimes we refer to someone experiencing a psychotic break as a person who has snapped. Actually, the evidence suggests that it is not a snap at all. It's more of a slide.

During mine, I wondered if I had it all wrong. Maybe I was never raped. I've been accused of being overly dramatic my entire life. Stop being such an actress, all the adults would say. Booze and drugs were involved. Often, I was drugged without consent. My memory is unreliable. I'm a loser. I'm a shit ass Orca loser.

(And from this point on, things become hard to describe. The closest I can approximate is to suggest imagining a confusion that leads to a sense of total obliteration. During my slide, I dream of Diderot's grave thief. I never see his face, only a close-up of his shoe as it slips in curdled corpse rot, impressing the marrow-colored paste between the tiles of sanctuary flooring. I think a lot about how Diderot once bitterly complained, "One wants some contrast, which breaks up the clear white light and makes it iridescent.")

Though unable to locate current information on his life, El Paso isn't that big of a place. My guess is that, once on the ground, it would take me no more than three days to locate him. I know the shithole places to look. Then again, why not leave the detective work up to a real detective? I could then slide into town for my reservation with its complimentary breakfast and await the intel.

Having secured the PI's report, I can pick my interrupting moment. And when I do, I won't be interested in talking. Though I suspect that Raper will. I also suspect that he will attempt to seduce me. This is how God works, he'd say. The last time we were together he prophesized just such an event. I guess I'm not sure what would happen at our reunion. I wonder what it would be like to kill him.

I'd be a tool-free killer. I don't want to open the body. When I imagine killing him, I see myself laying hands on him. Like the faith healers of my childhood who would lay hands on a janky human as they channeled the Holy Spirit into them. Except in this case, obviously, I would not be healing him. Or, I would be "healing" him.

For sure, he should die. We all should, a mercy. But I don't think he should get to have a rancher with a swimming pool. I don't think he should get to have a wooden sign upon which is painted *Live, Love, Laugh* in a remodeled open-floor concept suffering from gilded TJ Maxx elements. But the fact is that he has these things. And more. He has a lot of shit, including a convertible and a new amp.

I don't know what to do about it. It is one of the many feelings that happen in one's life after rape. This sense of not knowing what to do about any of it. The blinking hole that watches.

And this is the part where raped people might go into repetition. As if the repetition, built out in all directions, becomes a thing that is doing something. But what is it doing? Frying the main frame or framing an attempt out of the neuro-swell of one's own sweating brain loops. I don't even know how to end this piece of writing. Another feeling that happens in life after rape. The sense that you don't know how to end anything or that things don't end. The terrible, smooth underbelly of ongoingness.

Which brings up another aspect of life after rape: the unforgiving public.

How do you solve a problem like Maria? I would not know. Growing up, it was my grandmother who had the television, and every year when *The Sound of Music* aired on the local station, we were not allowed to watch it because my grandmother hated Julie Andrews, whom she considered an adventurous prude, a category of women she despised.

In the weeks leading up to the movie, the commercials would begin. I recall my grandmother sitting crisply in her orange Sear's recliner smoking a cigarette, sneering in disgust as a lithe Andrews twirled in an Alpine meadow. I have still never seen *The Sound of Music* despite my preoccupation with nuns, and it is my understanding Julie Andrews played one, or a former one. And though I have never seen this movie I feel I know the story: a woman in child-like love with God is reprieved from the nunnery because she has been selected for romantic love. God approves. It was, in fact, *jazz hands*, His idea.

How do you solve a problem like Maria? is also a repeated pun in the religious blogosphere concerning a different Maria, Maria Teresa Goretti, who was eleven years old at the time of her death in 1902. Half a century later, Maria was the youngest person ever to be canonized as a saint by the Catholic Church. Another first: present at her beatification, both the saint's mother and her murderer. Maria Goretti is the patron saint of sexual assault and rape victims. You might say that she is the patron saint of the #MeToo movement.

There are numerous conflicting narratives concerning Maria's life and death. In early accounts, she is raped to death. Once canonized, the story shifts: Maria dies "intact," a virgin who, while successfully repelling sexual intercourse, shares the gospel with her rapist-killer.

About Maria, some things, however, are established. We know that after her attack she was taken hours away to the nearest hospital. There surgeons noted that she was raped, choked, and stabbed 14 times with a ten-inch awl-like instrument, with wounds penetrating her throat, heart, lungs, and diaphragm. We know that she underwent surgery without anes-thesia (the hospital was apparently all out). We know that the electric lights she saw in the operating theatre were the first (and last) she saw in her life. As she died, Maria gave a statement to the Chief of Police in which she named her attacker, Alessandro Serenelli, whom, she said, had attempted to rape her on several prior occasions. We know that Maria's mother was a widow with lots of kids and, having fallen on hard times, moved her family in with another struggling family in the rural Italian countryside in an effort to eke out an existence working the fields. That other family was the Serenellis and Alessandro was the twenty-something son of this family. Following the death of Maria, Alessandro was tried, convicted, and sentenced to 30 years in prison.

In some stories, Maria's mother and older siblings are working in the fields as she stays behind to tend to her youngest sibling, still in his diapers, when Alessandro makes his lethal approach. In some stories, Maria's mother pimps her daughter out to Alessandro on the ruse of sending the girl to his room to "mend his buttonhole." In this version, Maria pleads with her mother not to enter Alessandro's bedchamber, at which point her mother loses her temper and hits Maria on the head with a shoe.

Regardless, once in prison Alessandro strikes up a friendship with a local bishop, one Monsignor Blandini. Eventually Alessandro tells Blandini that Maria appears to him at night and that she forgives him. Well, someone should tell the Pope. And so it is that Alessandro is eventually released from prison. He is placed with the Order of Friars Minor Capuchin, where he became an enthusiastic gardener and received housing, meals, and health care until his death at 87 years of age in 1970.

If you spend any time researching Maria Goretti you quickly learn that she is a controversial saint. The arguments about who and what she stands for are heated for those invested in the conversation. The Catholic Church has largely co-opted Maria to represent chastity. In this scenario, Maria is the ideal daughter at a Purity Ball, where, on repeat, she makes a pledge to remain a virgin until marriage under her father's approving eye. A few feminist thinkers have attempted to reclaim Maria from this yoke and, in this sense, she is recast, but subversively so.

How do you solve a problem like Maria?

In 2004 the schoolgirls of St. Maria Goretti High School for Girls in South Philly made the local news. Since the start of the school year, a man (later identified as Rudy Susando) had been showing up on school property and exposing himself. By mid-October the girls tired of his presence. One day Rudy whipped out his dick as per usual, but this time a group of twenty-five to thirty girls were waiting for the routine to begin.

The girls encircled him. Surprised, Rudy stuffed his dick back in his pants and took his exit. The girls followed. He picked up his pace. They picked up their pace. Rudy began to sprint, then run. The girls did the same. And they tracked him until they overtook him and forced him to the ground. According to witness statements, due to the brutality of the incident, bystanders did not wish to intervene. Finally someone called the cops and Rudy was taken to the hospital where he was treated for injuries, notably to his mouth, as the girls had kicked in his teeth. He was eventually sentenced on 13 counts of indecent exposure, open lewdness, corrupting minors, and stalking.

I have gone over and over this event in my mind. To understand this scene I enlist the help of my friend Bo, a filmmaker and devout attendant to Saint Maria Goretti. We discuss writing a screenplay about Maria Goretti. There is a 2003 Italian made-for-TV movie based on her life, which I have watched though I don't understand Italian. I know, however, that our project will be quite different. In this extended scene, for example, we will artistically reveal how Maria Goretti enters the girls under her patronage. Once possessed, all of the girls will simultaneously open their mouths wide in silence. And then close them. And open them. And so on. The only sound, the brace architecture of gummy mouths in process. And in the mouths, butterflies. Some escape in-tact. Most get clogged at the congested exit valve so that eventually the girls' mouths are stuffed open with suffering butterflies and their eyes roll to the backs of their heads.

Is what these girls did a good or bad thing? Or, was it a nuanced, complicated thing that troubles the binary, and if so, how do we get comfortable not knowing?

How do you catch a cloud and pin it down?

In 2019 Julie Andrews, who famously played Maria Von Trapp in *The Sound of Music*, released her memoir, *Home Work*. She writes about her stepfather, Ted Andrews, a vaudeville performer, known to Julie as Pop. It was Ted Andrews who first noticed Julie's incredible talent and brought her on stage to perform alongside him. She also writes about how, starting at age nine, she was forced to share a bed with him and thus learned of his predatory inclinations.

In one famous story about Maria Goretti, halfway through her surgery (the one without anesthesia), the surgeon says to her, "Maria, think of me in Paradise," to which she replies, "Well, who knows which of us is going to be there first," to which he knowingly replies, "You, Maria."

I can imagine writing as a Eucharistic event. In the mouth. In house. I can imagine a sentence which punches me in the stomach. Noli me tangere: touch me not. Words said by Jesus to Mary Magdalene

when she encountered him post-crucifixion in a passage of writing considered to be some of the most difficult to interpret in the whole of the New Testament. The dominant prevailing historic read of Mary Magdalene is that she has a credibility issue.

Over twenty years ago, I spent four years studying and extrapolating this verse: the seventeenth of the twentieth chapter of the Book of John, the most Gnostic of the canonized gospels, and using acute stitches, relating my analysis to issues of proclamation rooted through Eucharistic traditions. The result was a 278-page (unpublished) monograph painfully titled, *Noli Me Tangere: The Disbelief of Women's Proclamations as it Relates to Eucharistic Celebrations and Bodily Sovereignty within Contemporary Hermeneutics.*

It is a book that outlines a feminist Hermeneutics of touching and reading, two gestures springing from the same root. For example, when a woman can't touch the body of Christ (Noli me tangere), history bears out that in short order, she can't touch the other great corpse: the Word that is God, the Biblical text. Which is to say, she is not allowed to read it out loud, by herself, within the church, with recognized authority. Which, in turn, stripped women of political rights and bodily sovereignty. Here we find ancient debates concerning women being able to control their own bodies (reproductive rights) as well as the (still, in many places) hotly contested issue of the ordination of women into the priesthood.

G/host. The old-timey story of how a ghost becomes a host (that, once in your mouth, turns back into a body). Words are haunted by bodies and bodies are full of words, which are also ghosts. It is this communion-juncture that so often undergirds the experience of writing for me.

I once asked Joan of Arc about not being believed. We were having a cigarette between shifts. "Listen," Joan said, while sucking down a Virginia Slim. "Imagine screaming: I am on fire. Imagine your blood boiling. I'll tell you what," she continued, "I felt like goddamned Carrie at the prom free bleeding, the stigmata in overdrive, like having your period out of your eye balls or whatever."

Imagine screaming in someone's face, but the someone does not hear you. Imagine the isolation you might feel. You might begin to wonder if you are a ghost. And this is why no one can hear you screaming.

From somewhere else in this essay, my dead grandmother lights a cigarette in her orange Sears recliner and says that where her family was from in Scotland they had a name for that sort of woman, the Keening Woman. In her body she held the Spirit of Lamentation, and it was her burden to vocalize it on behalf of the village.

We went to the tree centering the village. We plucked its shiny apples. We sank teeth into Eden's mealy cud. We returned to the fields. We gossiped. We masturbated. We don't know what to tell you. We owned things. We used the shunt. We heard cicada zzz-zzzzing the warble. We repurposed unmarked boxes. We tried out for varsity cheerleader. We said, "Nights like this remind us of pearls." We took vows. We cut the rut where language flows. We generated municipal paper letterhead supply. August the twenty-eighth, nineteen hundred and *Dear Mr.*_____, I have been remiss in responding to your note. We slouched in sweat and wanted. We eyed the emptied motes. We imagined the shadow of the host. We loosened the filament. We saw a red bird dead in snow. We practiced difficult to pronounce names in advance of the presentation. We edged our tongues in silver during death themes. We became haunted by an annual pink ghost. The haunting was within. We lazily strolled the bloodlines. We kept track of time. We have only one minute less than one now. We double-tied the ribbon. We named the field Elysium. We knew what happened in that house. At the end of that lonely forsaken gravel road. Within the rusted frame. So pack it down with sugar, sugar weight it till it drowns. A village knows what a village knows.

It turns out, I got to see an Orca in real life. On a handsome vessel off the coast of the most Southern tip of South Africa on a gorgeous day, a privilege made possible by an academic job, originally made possible by my need to survive.

I'm pretty goddamned sure it was while eating a Piggly Wiggly Bear Claw that I decided I needed a plan to get the fuck out of where I was.

I came up with two options: a misguided fantasy that Metallica's tour bus would roll through my small town and break down during which time I would marry a band member (any = fine), or I'd get a scholarship. I didn't fully grasp what a scholarship was, but I understood even then and while in the throes of the rural Mississippi public school system, that education was potentially a ticket out, something I now understand was not true for other girls, especially black and brown girls.

When Tara Westover's memoir, *Educated*, came out, people told me I had to read it. I skulked around its presence and finally did. I identified with much in that book, and I had big issues with that book.

My friend who told me about the egg sac harvesting friend did, too. While our kids smeared pasta across their faces, she spoke to my own feelings when she described the ways she felt Westover weaponizes education and also rolls with so much unchecked ableism.

It isn't that education is a bad ticket out of hell, it's just that when you believe that the transport vessel is so good that God can't even sink it, then you are in real trouble.

In my reading of Westover's book, education fulfills its class fantasy by finally eradicating all traces of the accent within. No one has to feel anything except exceptional. The mythical white knight of white feminism is cast as the ivory light of the tower of academia.

When I got my academic job, there was a sense among my family and community that I had made it to solid ground. At last, I was far away from the hard times. Everyone expected me to thrive, and everything in my new life was set up so that I might.

I often think about how puzzling I must have seemed to the people in my new world. I was unable to accept the invitation to connection. Paradoxically, the stability I had labored to achieve made it possible for me to inhabit a life that was safe enough to feel the depths of my trauma, which I hadn't intended to do, but there I was, unraveling. Like a lot of academics I know, I had astute survival skills, but I did not have the skills I needed to thrive. And what happened next was that I lost the plot, literally and figuratively. I began a shame spiral that took me to sad and dangerous places.

Later I learned from a healer that there is a term for the seeming paradox of, at last, pitching yourself into a stable situation, only to self-sabotage or otherwise break-down. This, she said, is a healing crisis. The individual intent on healing, will, in the end, feel and express every information-packed wound. Past symptoms, repressed sensations, and unacknowledged trauma will rise up even as you prepare to relax. Living, she concluded, is not for the faint of heart. And then she laughed. She laughed so hard I felt embarrassed for her so I joined in. Then I was really laughing. Later that day I thought, for the first time in a long time, maybe there was hope for a person like me.

In the hour between night and morning, a dream sets in. I'm driving my step-father's '78 Dodge Charger down a hell-hot highway. Then, thanks to a semi that slams on the breaks, an accident. My car is propelled many miles down into a valley where a small, isolated village exists. The car accident has caused considerable damage to the village center. People are upset, and justice was going to be served. I stood accused of Utter Discord, a grave offense. The more I proclaim my innocence, the less I am believed. The less I am believed. I am burned from the accident and when I remove my clothing to reveal these wounds, there are intricate, shifting designs. On my arm, a detailed portrait of a tree connecting heaven and earth. Meanwhile, the villagers prepare for my execution by gathering kindling.

I will myself awake into a cold, sweating form. Early light diffuses through the curtains. I hear my wife sleeping and, from the other room, my infant daughter's sound machine casting its thunderstorms. Then I hear a voice. It comes from my side of the bed. It approaches.

The voice has a long, thin tongue, which enters my ear canal.

The voice is a cavern, which holds other voices. Three come together and flap within the mother voice, saying, "The ancient terror of this life, and every life before, is of not being believed."

My rapist bought a house with a swimming pool in El Paso, and when I found out, reality broke and not merely because I was surprised to see him, but because for years I had believed he was dead and buried in a Potter's Field on the Texas/Louisiana border.

I had every reason to believe he was dead, including the fact that I had known him. It would surprise absolutely no one that he would turn up dead. Furthermore, I believed he was dead because his death story as told to me was so fixed in its details, it seemed impossible that it could be anything except true. Shit stuffed in a murder-fucked mouth in a meth motel etc. My source of information was close to him and would have known. It was she who not only told me of his death, but claimed to have experienced its visceral aftermath. Upon seeing a somewhat recent image of him very much alive in front of the rancher, I realized she had not, for reasons that remain unclear, told the truth. In that cruel and strange moment, I felt my heart drop from my chest into the bayou and anything that drops there can never be recovered through normal ways. Only spiritual and/or illegal ways.

I did not want to use diversion as a primary narrative technique in this essay. As if to suggest: these tiny veined narrative departures have, all along, really been vehicles delivering you into the wide river of truth that firms up this story, whatever this story is. Whatever the truth is.

But it turns out cleverness, in the end, does rule.

I've been writing this essay so long that the fake-ass story of his death is becoming true. The liar, turns out, was a prophet. Prophets are often depicted as laughing.

Personally, I feel like I can never stop thinking about resurrection. Resurrection sickness. I get bouts. A pitch-dark sphere pushing out a flower at double-bloom, which retracts, and then blooms again. It smells of bitter chocolate mixed with menstrual blood and moss.

"Listen, if you stick around on the Wheel long enough every lie becomes true," Joan says. "It is, literally," she emphasizes with a dramatic exhale of cig smoke, "how the universe works." I won't pretend I understand everything Joan says. Later she texts:

"After work do you want to become each other?"

The resurrection of my rapist is also a re-inscription of his demise, the void's flower face that won't stop throwing up on the edge of anguish. And this essay is an abandoned church. And I'm in attendance.

"Well," says the spirit who lives in my basement laundry room, "maybe you shouldn't write a goddamned essay about it." Exactly, I nod. Why write an essay on a topic about which I have nothing interesting to say? "Actually," the spirit continues, "I've been meaning to tell you something. That particular repetition isn't really working in the piece at this point. It isn't that you don't have anything interesting to say about rape. It's that you feel like you are only allowed to write about it if you are making a worthy contribution to the subject or to the field of literature. Meanwhile that guy got a sweet-ass rancher. Frankly, it just feels sad."

I would here add that diversion's relation to avoidance is well documented. We were diverted from traffic, the scene of the crime, the truth, the Angel of Death passed over. It feels useful to recall that deep within the guts of its etymology "divert" includes notions of changing destinations all together.

In fact, in every iteration of the word's history, the notion of "the turn" shimmers into focus. A turn, wrong or otherwise. Turn, a word that belongs to both moon and lathe, that tool which mimics the moon's rotations. One thing I appreciate about "the turn" is that it inherently rejects productivity without excluding fecundity. This essay isn't working towards anything. It is a being-with. It is trying to be with something.

It is trying to do this through spider eggs and child saints. It dips a child's hand into a saint pit of eggs and lifts the spiders up.

Who is the spirit living in the basement laundry room? you may wonder. Larry gives advice. I've never known a spirit to give advice until I met Larry. He sits on a stool in the corner, slouched, like Rodin's *Thinker*, a cliché, but accurate. Larry is outfitted from head to toe in smart denim. It's a look. He touches his mustache a lot. You can tell Larry really cared for his mustache when he was alive. Whenever I question Larry about his life or the manner of his death, he becomes enveloped in thought, as if trying to remember something. And Larry is bummed the fuck out. He is seriously down in the dumps. He's as blue as they get.

Talking to Larry began as a way to put myself at ease. If I had to be in the laundry room for more than a minute I'd start talking to Larry, which is how I started giving Larry updates on my writing, including this essay. Larry has grown tired of this essay about rape. Me, too! I say to Larry as I overzealously fold adorable holiday-themed pillowcases created by my mother-in-law.

Dusty Rose, says Larry. Then he becomes lost in himself, stilled in a ghosty fog with the exception of an occasional agitated twitch.

I think that Larry will eventually remember whatever it is he can't recall and I think when he does he'll disappear from my basement.

I wish a rape was more like a ghost. That after some process of recognition it would, at last, disappear. That it would, as they say, go into the light.

Larry will move on, and will he ever even think about me?

But I will always think about Larry.

How does this essay end? I've been writing this essay so long, I can tell you. Unable to trust my original source, I eventually have a dream in which I'm seated across from a woman who slides her business card across the table to where I am seated. On one side, a phone number. On the other, a single word: Truth. After this dream, I consult a professional and over time, she makes several reports. Fast forward to the final:

In the end, my rapist does lose the rancher, the swimming pool, and the family. It is a terrible story, in fact. An ending happening in real time. My rapist's death is near. He is sick and won't improve. He is alone in the shitty motel of his skull.

Julia says maybe you write an essay about rape to realize that it is an essay that will not end. An essay is a living document like a person is a living archive. Nothing ends it. Not even publication ends it. She wonders: What are we, if not gathering? We will find a place where one can rest, she tells me, we will find a place where a story can rest.

Kristen feels a lot of the essays that she's read about rape have a sort of either/or narrative. *It destroyed me* or *now I'm stronger*. Or *it was a dark time* but *now I'm better*. She is grateful for any person who takes on this topic and tries to make sense of it. And, she says, she desires most the essay that takes on all of the gray areas of destruction and survival. The clingy stickiness of it all. Like, she clarifies, the pearl-colored blood of milkweed.

Katie Jean says that a truth-telling essay reveals broken systemic structures that contribute to/ contain/define/allow systemically fucked acts to occur and keep reoccurring. This goes beyond "telling my story" or "telling a story" and is about engaging with injustices and creating space to do the social justice work of continuing to fight entrenched trauma-generating systems.

Lately, she says, she can't stop thinking of something that comes up with her students in the fiction workshop, something that she is both for and against, but something her students keep talking about: how most everything in a story should give information (either in absentia or outright) or should, somehow, move the plot forward. And what is occurring to her through these conversations is that, by shining a light on something like rape, the cultural conversation is moved forward in a larger way. It gives the chorus power. And with power, comes strength. Maybe, she says, something will change, or someone will listen, or we will listen to each other.

Teresa says she has been thinking about what an essay about rape is supposed to do since she began to write so: always. An essay about rape is not supposed to do anything, she says. Essays, like all writing, like other beings, simply exist in various stages of growth.

She says that when we talk about "sharing our story," the underlying assumption is often something like:

hearing my story will help others heal from theirs. This is true and not-true. True because hearing others' stories often brings our stories into clearer focus by piercing the cloak of shame that surrounds our abusive experience. Not true because healing isn't a point to be reached, but a process, ever unfolding.

The brain will only let us see that which we are ready to face; the concentrated focus of an essay—the deep stillness and inner knowing felt during the writing process—creates the conditions for seeing, witnessing, our own pain. It creates the conditions for spirit to show up (where two or more are gathered).

She says that in metabolizing this emotional reality through the first two bodies (the writer, the text), it is prepared for a third body (the reader). This can be a gift of divine love. (A trinity re-imagined).

The sucky paradox about any kind of abuse is the way the traumatic event absolutely isn't the victim's fault even as she is ultimately responsible for her own healing process.

The person, she continues, most touched by the essay on rape is the essayist. It is her healing, first and foremost, that's at stake.

The sentences my friends offer move through my interior and are made pliable. I weave these strands into a breathing basket. I imagine I am reweaving the passageway for neurotransmission. I massage each strand with rose oil, whispering to future light impulses: *don't drop the signal.*

ACKNOWLEDGMENTS

The author wishes to thank Gina Abelkop, Sarah Boyer, Teresa Carmody, Julie Carr, Kelly Corbin, Julia Cohen, Jen Denrow, Steven Dunn, Ron Estrada, Mindy Gates, Roger Green, Hannah Rae Hegnauer, Laird Hunt, Vincent James, Diane Kimmell, Bo McGuire, Kristen E. Nelson, Bailey Pittinger, Michelle Puckett, Frankie Rollins, Katie Jean Shinkle, Eleni Sikelianos, Heather Cathleen Dunaway Smith, and Magdalena Zurawaski. I am very thankful for Ryan Rivas and the amazing team at Burrow Press. Thank you for the conversations, which are really temples in which I live.

Images from the Imaginary Anatomy series
by H.C. Dunaway Smith

ABOUT THE AUTHOR / ARTIST

Selah Saterstrom is the author of the novels *Slab*, *The Meat and Spirit Plan*, and *The Pink Institution* (all published by Coffee House Press) as well as the award-winning book of essays, *Ideal Suggestions: Essays in Divinatory Poetics* (published by Essay Press). She is the Director of Creative Writing at the University of Denver and she co-directs Four Queens, a platform for creative and divinatory arts. She lives in Denver with wife, writer and book designer Hannah Rae Hegnauer, and their daughter. Visit her at selahsaterstrom.org.

H.C. Dunaway Smith is an interdisciplinary artist and storyteller that combines illustration, music, animation, branching narratives, and mixed reality techniques into interactive experiences that explore existence—what it is to "be." Raised in the forests of Poetry, Texas, she brings her life-long fascination with nature and science into her artwork, exploring everything from the micro to the macro. She hopes to foster authentic, personal connections by creating a dialog between art and audience.

Printed in the USA
CPSIA information can be obtained
at www.ICGtesting.com
JSHW072037210823
46922JS00010B/141